Spotlight on Poetry

Poems Around the World

Contents

Everybody Rap	3
Poetry Jump-Up	4
The Panther	7
De	8
The River	10
Sensemaya: A Chant For Killing A Snake	12
The Storm	14
Moon	15
The Distant Talking Drum	16
In the Garden	18
Can You?	19
The Picnic in Jammu	22
The Door	24
The Father's Song	26
Isn't My Name Magical?	28
The Dream Keeper	30
Glossary	31
Index by title	32
Index by first line	32

Collected by Brian Moses and David Orme

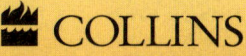

Collins

Acknowledgements

Whilst every effort has been made to contact the copyright-holders and to secure the necessary permission to reprint these selections, this has not proved to be possible in every case.

'Poetry Jump-Up' by John Agard from Get Back Pimple (Viking/Puffin, 1996), reprinted by kind permission of the author c/o Caroline Sheldon Literary Agency; 'The Panther' by Rainer Maria Rilke, translated by Jessie Lemont, from Out of the Ark (Columbia University Press); 'De' and 'The River' by Valerie Bloom, reprinted by permission of the author; 'Can You?' by Nicolás Guillén from Can I Buy a Slice of Sky?: Poems from Black, Asian and American Indian Cultures, edited by Grace Nichols (Penguin Books, 1991); 'Isn't My Name Magical?' by James Berry from A Caribbean Dozen, edited by John Agard and Grace Nichols (Walker Books, 1994), reprinted by kind permission of the author; 'Sensemaya: A Chant For Killing A Snake' by Nicolás Guillén, translated by G. R. Coulthard, from You'll Love This Stuff: Poems from Many Cultures, edited by Morag Styles (Cambridge University Press, 1987); 'The Distant Talking Drum' by Isaac Olaleye from The Distant Talking Drum (Boyds Mills Press, Inc., 1995), text copyright © 1995 by Isaac Olaleye, reprinted by permission of the publisher; 'The Dream Keeper' by Langston Hughes from Collected Poems of Langston Hughes (Alfred A. Knopf, 1994), reprinted by permission of David Higham Associates; 'The Moon' by Li Bai from Maples in the Mist: Children's Poems from the T'ang Dynasty, translated by M. Ho (William Morrow, 1997); 'The Door' by Miroslav Holub, translated by Ian Milner and George Theiner, from Selected Poems (Penguin Books, 1967); 'Everybody Rap' by Su Andi, reprinted by permission of the author.

The publishers would be pleased to rectify any omissions in the above list brought to their notice at the earliest opportunity.

Published by Collins Educational
An imprint of HarperCollinsPublishers
77-85 Fulham Palace Road
Hammersmith
London W6 8JB

www.CollinsEducation.com
On-line support for schools and colleges

© HarperCollinsPublishers 1999

First published 1999

Reprinted 2000

Reprinted 0 9 8 7 6 5 4

ISBN 0 00 310 340 4

All rights reserved. No part of this publication may be reproduced, stored in a retrieval system or transmitted in any form or by any other means – electronic, mechanical, photocopying, recording or otherwise – without the prior written permission of the Publisher or a licence permitting restricted copying in the United Kingdom issued by the Copyright Licensing Agency Ltd, 90 Tottenham Court Road, London W1P OLP.

Designed by Clare Truscott and Kate Roberts
Cover Design by Clare Truscott and Kate Roberts
Illustrations by Helen Cann, Michael Charlton, Abigail Conway, Emma Garner, Tracey Morgan, Anthony Morris, Deborah Pook, Tina Schneider, Jan Smith, Holly Swain, Joanna Troughton, Lisa Williams

Printed and bound in Great Britain by Scotprint, Haddington

Collins Educational would like to thank the following teachers and consultants who contributed to the research of this series:

Mrs J. Bibby (St Paul's C of E Primary); Jason Darley, Liz Hooley (Jessop Primary School); Mrs M.G. Farnell (High Meadow First School); Alison Lewis; Chris Lutrario; Lesley Moores (Princess Royal Primary School); Sheila Stamp (Castle Lower School); Sally Prendergrast (Brooke Hill School); Jenny Ransom; Jill Walkinton; Sue Webb; Michael Webster (Castle Lower School); Jill Wells (St Andrews CE Primary School).

Everybody Rap

Can you do a rap?
    Can you do a rap?
Can you make a rhyme?
    Can you make a rhyme?
Can you link up words,
    Can you link up words,
To help me blow my mind?
    To help me blow my mind?

    Poetry is the thing that we can do
    To show that there's no difference
    Between me and you.

Black and white are all the same
And those that say different are mad insane.

    Do you agree?
    I said do you agree?
    If you agree,
    Say yowl to me.

Su Andi

Poetry Jump-Up

Tell me if ah seeing right
Take a look down de street

Words dancin
words dancin
till dey sweat
words like fishes
jumpin out a net
words wild and free
joinin de poetry revelry
words back to back
words belly to belly

Come on everybody
come and join de poetry band
dis is poetry carnival
dis is poetry bacchanal
when inspiration call
take yu pen in yu hand
if yu dont have a pen
take yu pencil in yu hand
if you dont have a pencil
what the hell

so long de feeling start to swell
just shout de poem out

Words jumping off de page
tell me if Ah seeing right
words like birds
jumpin out a cage
take a look down de street
words shakin dey waist
words shakin dey bum
words wit black skin
words wit white skin
words wit brown skin
words wit no skin at all
words huggin up words
an saying I want to be a poem today
rhyme or no rhyme
I is a poem today
I mean to have a good time

Words feelin hot hot hot
big words feelin hot hot hot
lil words feelin hot hot hot
even sad words cant help
tappin dey toe
to de riddum of de poetry band

Dis is poetry carnival
dis is poetry bacchanal
so come on everybody
join de celebration
all yu need is plenty perspiration
an a little inspiration
plenty perspiration
an a little inspiration

John Agard

The Panther

His weary glance, from passing by the bars,
Has grown into a dazed and vacant stare;
It seems to him there are a thousand bars
And out beyond those bars the empty air.

The pad of his strong feet, that ceaseless sound
Of supple tread behind the iron bands,
Is like a dance of strength circling around,
While in the circle, stunned, a great will stands.

But there are times the pupils of his eyes
Dilate, the strong limbs stand alert, apart,
Tense with the flood of visions that arise
Only to sink and die within his heart.

Rainer Maria Rilke
trans. Jessie Lemont

De

De snow, de sleet, de lack o' heat,
De runny nose, de frostbite,
De lip turn blue, de cold, "ACHOO!"
De fire dat won't ignite,

De creakin' knee, de misery,
De joint dem all rheumatic,
De icy bed, (de blanket dead)
De burs' pipe in de attic.

De window a-shake, de glass near break,
De wind dat cut like razor,
De wonderin' why you never buy
De window from dat double-glazer.

De heavy coat, zip to de throat,
De nose an' ears all pinky,
De weepin' sky, de clothes can't dry,
De day dem long an' inky.

De icy road, de heavy load,
De las' minute Christmus shoppin'
De cuss an' fret 'cause you feget
De ribbon an' de wrappin'.

De mud, de grime, de slush, de slime,
De place gloomy since November,
De sinkin' heart, is jus' de start, o'
De wintertime,
December.

Valerie Bloom

The River

The River's a wanderer,
A nomad, a tramp,
He never chooses one place
To set up his camp.

The River's a winder,
Through valley and hill
He twists and he turns'
He just cannot be still.

The River's a hoarder
And he buries down deep
Those little treasures
That he wants to keep.

The River's a baby,
He gurgles and hums,
And sounds like he's happily
Sucking his thumbs.

The River's a singer,
As he dances along,
The countryside echoes
The notes of his song.

The River's a monster
Hungry and vexed,
He's gobbled up trees
And he'll swallow you next.

Valerie Bloom

Sensemaya: A Chant For Killing A Snake

Mayombe-bombe-mayombe!
Mayombe-bombe-mayombe!
Mayombe-bombe-mayombe!

The snake has eyes of glass;
the snake comes and coils itself round a pole;
with eyes of glass, round a pole,
with his eyes of glass.
The snake walks without legs;
the snake hides in the grass;
walking he hides in the grass
walking without legs.

Mayombe-bombe-mayombe!
Mayombe-bombe-mayombe!
Mayombe-bombe-mayombe!

If you hit him with an axe he will die.
Hit him hard!
Do not hit him with your foot, he will bite,
do not hit him with your foot, he is going away!

Sensemaya, the snake,
Sensemaya.

Sensemaya, with his eyes,
Sensemaya.
Sensemaya, with his tongue,
Sensemaya.
Sensemaya, with his mouth,
Sensemaya –.

Dead snake cannot eat;
dead snake cannot hiss;
cannot walk,
cannot run.
Dead snake cannot look;
dead snake cannot drink;
cannot breathe,
cannot bite.

Mayombe-bombe-mayombe!
Sensemaya, the snake –
Mayombe-bombe-mayombe!
Sensemaya, it is still –
Mayombe-bombe-mayombe!
Sensemaya, the snake –
Mayombe-bombe-mayombe!
Sensemaya, it is dead.

Nicolás Guillén
trans. G.R. Coulthard

The Storm

Without warning a snake of black
cloud rises in the sky.
It hisses as it runs and spreads its hood.
The moon goes out, the mountain is dark.
Far away is heard the shout of the demon.

Up rushes the storm a moment after
Rattling an iron chain in its teeth
The mountain suddenly lifts its
Trunk to the heavens
And the lake roars like a wild beast.

Ashok B. Raha
trans. Lila Ray

Moon

When I was little
I thought the moon was a white jade plate,
Or maybe a mirror in Heaven
Flying through the blue clouds.

Li Bai

The Distant Talking Drum

From deep in the rain forest
The sound of a distant talking drum I hear –
Far away, far away.
For me it calls.
Clearly it calls
For me to dance,
For men to dance,
For women to dance,
For children to dance.

And the sound of the distant drum
Echoes through the rain forest.
The distant talking drum
Is calling across the mighty rain forest
For me to come,
For me to dance.
Now the sound of sweet songs
I hear.
Beautifully they flow!

And the distant talking drum
Is still calling
Far away, far away.
Clearly it calls
For me to come,
For me to dance.
So across the rain forest,
The wide, wild, and wonderful rain forest,
I go!

Isaac Olaleye

In the Garden

Two ink-blue butterflies,
Their probosces curled,
Slumber on a sunflower
Like moored yachts
In a quiet harbour
With gaudy sails unfurled.

A great bumble-bee goes humming by
Like a Zeppelin in the sky,
Encasing the night in each eye.

Rupendra Guha Majumdar

Can You?

Can you sell me the air as it slips through your fingers
As it slaps at your face and untidies your hair?
Perhaps you could sell me fivepennyworth of wind
or more, perhaps sell me a storm?
Perhaps the elegant air
you would sell me, that air
(not all of it) which trips around
your garden, from corolla to corolla
in your garden for the birds
tenpence worth of elegant air?
   The air spins and goes by
   in a butterfly
   Belongs to no one, no one.

Can you sell me the sky
the sky sometimes blue
or grey as well sometimes
a strip of your sky
the bit you think you bought with the trees
of your garden, as one buys the roof with the house?

Can you sell me a dollar
of sky, two miles
of sky, a slice, whatever you can
of your sky?
    The sky is in the clouds
    The clouds go by
    Belong to no one, no one.

Can you sell me the rain, the water
given you by your tears, and moistening your tongue?
Can you sell me a dollar of water
from a spring, a gravid cloud
crinkly and soft as a sheep
or perhaps rainwater up in the mountains
or the water from puddles
left for the dogs
or a stretch of sea, maybe a lake,
a hundred dollars of lake?
    Water falls, rolls on.
    Water rolls on, goes by.
    Belongs to no one, no one.

Can you sell me the earth, the deep
night of the roots, teeth
of dinosaurs and the lime
dispersed from distant skeletons?
Can you sell me forests lying buried, birds that are dead
fishes of stone, the sulphur
of volcanoes, a thousand million years
twisting their way up? can you
sell me earth, can you
sell me earth, can you?
    Your earth is mine.
    Trodden by everyone's feet.
    Belongs to no one, no one.

Nicolás Guillén

The Picnic in Jammu

Uncle Ayub swung me round and round
till the horizon became a rail
banked high upon the Himalayas.
The trees signalled me past. I whistled,
shut my eyes through tunnels of the air.
The family laughed, watching me puff
out my muscles, healthily aggressive.

This was late summer, before the snows
come to Kashmir, this was picnic time.

Then, uncoupling me from the sky, he
plunged me into the river, himself
a bough with me dangling at its end.
I went purple as a plum. He reared
back and lowered the branch of his arm
to grandma who swallowed me with a kiss.
Laughter peeled away my goosepimples.

This was late summer, before the snows
come to Kashmir, this was picnic time.

After we'd eaten, he aimed grapes at
my mouth. I flung at him the shells of
pomegranates and ran off. He tracked
me down the river-bank. We battled,
melon-rind and apple-core our arms.
'You two!' grandma cried. 'Stop fighting, you'll
tire yourselves to death!' We didn't listen.

This was late summer, before the snows
come to Kashmir and end children's games.

Zulfikar Ghose

The Door

Go and open the door.
   Maybe outside there's
  a tree, or a wood,
  a garden,
  or a magic city.

Go and open the door.
   Maybe a dog's rummaging.
   Maybe you'll see a face,
or an eye,
or the picture
            of a picture.

Go and open the door.
  If there's a fog
  it will clear.

Go and open the door.
 Even if there's only
  the darkness ticking,
  even if there's only
  the hollow wind,
  even if
     nothing
          is there,
go and open the door.

At least
there'll be
a draught.

Miroslav Holub
trans. Ian Milner
and George Theiner

The Father's Song

Great snowslide,
Stay away from my igloo,
I have my four children and my wife;
They can never enrich you.

Strong snowslide
Roll past my weak house.
There sleep my dear ones in the world.
Snowslide, let their night be calm.

Sinister snowslide,
I just built an igloo here, sheltered from the wind.
It is my fault if it is put wrong.
Snowslide, hear me from your mountain.

Greedy snowslide,
There is enough to smash and smother.
Fall down over the ice,
Bury stones and cliffs and rocks.

Snowslide, I own so little in the world.
Keep away from my igloo, stop not our travels.
Nothing will you gain by our horror and death,
Mighty snowslide, mighty snowslide.

Little snowslide,
Four children and my wife are my whole world, all I own,
All I can lose, nothing can you gain.
Snowslide, save my house, stay on your summit.

Anon.

Isn't My Name Magical?

Nobody can see my name on me.
My name is inside
and all over me, unseen
like other people also keep it.
   Isn't my name magic?

My name is mine only.
It tells I am individual,
the only special person it shakes
when I'm wanted.

If I'm with hundreds of people
and my name gets called,
my sound switches me on to answer
like it was my human electricity.
   Isn't that magical?

My name echoes across playground,
it comes, it demands my attention.
I have to find out who calls,
who wants me for what.
My name gets blurted out in class,
it is a terror, at a bad time,
because somebody is cross.

My name gets called in a whisper
I am happy, because
my name may have touched me
with a loving voice.
    Isn't it all magic?

James Berry

The Dream Keeper

Bring me all of your dreams,
You dreamers,
Bring me all of your
Heart melodies
That I may wrap them
In a blue cloud-cloth
Away from the too-rough fingers
Of the world.

Langston Hughes

Glossary

Can You?
corolla   ring of petals inside a flower
gravid   pregnant
sulphur   a pale, yellow substance which burns with a blue flame and gives off a suffocating smell
trodden   the past tense of tread, to set down your foot or press or crush with it

In the Garden
encasing   confining
gaudy   tasteless
probosces   elongated part of insects' mouth, can also refer to elephants' trunk, etc.
slumber   sleep
unfurled   spread out
Zeppelin   large German airship

Isn't My Name Magical?
blurted   said something suddenly
unseen   something you haven't seen or cannot see

Poetry Jump-Up
bacchanal   reveller or revelry, riotous
revelry   people enjoying themselves in a riotous and festive way

The Door
draught   a current of cold air
rummaging   searching, moving things about carelessly

The Father's Song
enrich   improves the quality or value of something

igloo   a dome-shaped house built out of snow by the Inuit, or Eskimo, people
mighty   very powerful or strong
sinister   seeming harmful or evil
smother   to cover someone's face with something so that they cannot breathe
summit   peak, or top

The Panther
arise   when something, for example a problem, arises, it begins to exist, or to stand up from a sitting, kneeling or lying position
ceaseless   without stopping
supple   able to bend and move easily
tread   to set down your foot, press or crush with it

The Picnic in Jammu
banked high   high ground on each side of the river
horizon   the distant line where the sky seems to touch the land or sea
pomegranates   tropical fruit with hard rind and reddish insides with many seeds
reared   when a horse rears it raises the front part of its body, so that its front legs are in the air

The River
hoarder   someone who saves things even though they may no longer be useful

Index by title   page

Can You?	19
De	8
Everybody Rap	3
In the Garden	18
Isn't My Name Magical?	28
Moon	15
Poetry Jump-Up	4
Sensemaya: A Chant For Killing A Snake	12
The Distant Talking Drum	16
The Door	24
The Dream Keeper	30
The Father's Song	26
The Panther	7
The Picnic in Jammu	22
The River	10
The Storm	14

Index by first line   page

Bring me all of your dreams	30
Can you do a rap?	3
Can you sell me the air as it slips through your fingers	19
De snow, de sleet, de lack o' heat	8
From deep in the rain forest	16
Go and open the door	24
Great snowslide	26
His weary glance, from passing by the bars	7
Mayombe-bombe-mayombe!	12
Nobody can see my name on me	28
Tell me if ah seeing right	4
The River's a wanderer	10
Two ink-blue butterflies	18
Uncle Ayub swung me round and round	22
When I was little	15
Without warning a snake of black	14